PROSPERO'S LIBRARY

*The Book of Symbols*

# Dragons and Fabulous Beasts

## CHRONICLE BOOKS
### SAN FRANCISCO

First published in the United States in 1995 by Chronicle Books.

A DBP Book, conceived, edited and designed by
Duncan Baird Publishers
Castle House
75-76 Wells Street
London
W1P 3RE

Text: *Violet Wharton*
Design: *Karen Wilks*
Commissioned artwork: *Geoffrey Appleton*
Picture research: *Julia Brown*
Additional research: *Lucy Curtin*

1 3 5 7 9 10 8 6 4 2

Library of Congress Cataloging-in-Publication Data:
Dragons and fabulous beasts: a book of symbols.
p.   cm. — (Prospero's library)
ISBN 0-8118-1018-6
1. Animals, Mythical. 2. Dragons. I. Series.
GR825.D73   1995
398'.469—dc20                    94-37304
CIP

Distributed in Canada by Raincoast Books,
8680 Cambie Street, Vancouver, B.C. V6P 6M9

Chronicle Books
275 Fifth Street
San Francisco, California 94103

Printed in Hong Kong

# CONTENTS

### The universal dragon

### Beasts of the elements

### Beasts of myth and mystery

## The dragon of the cosmos

**M**ost commonly depicted as a great winged reptile, the dragon inspires fascination, fear or reverence in almost every culture of the world. Fierce and untamed, protector and destroyer, it embodies the elemental creative and degenerative forces of the universe, a symbol of both cosmic order and disorder. Many peoples believe that a rainbow is a giant dragon or serpent that encircles the earth, dividing the ordered material world from the unseen chaos beyond.

**Uroboros**
The uroboros, the dragon or serpent swallowing its own tail (above), is an ancient symbol found in places as far apart as West Africa and Central America. With its beginning and end at the same point, it represents the eternal cosmic cycle of destruction and simultaneous regeneration.

## The churning of the ocean

The energy emanating from the coiled, writhing dragon is a potent creative force. In Hindu myth, the gods and demons coiled Vasuki, a giant many-headed dragon, around Mount Mandara to churn the ocean. In doing so they created the Sun, the Moon, the goddess of fortune, and the elixir of immortality.

## Thor and the World Dragon

In Norse cosmology the earth was encompassed by a turbulent sea, the domain of the poisonous World Dragon. The god Thor failed to catch the dragon using an ox head as bait (above, right), but later killed the beast at the apocalyptic battle of Ragnarok.

## The dragon of nature

For the ancients, the four elements from which everything was formed – earth, air, fire and water – were symbolically conjoined in the dragon, which dwells in the earth or the waters, flies through the air and breathes fire. In the East, the dragon's energy binds all the phenomena of nature, bringing benevolent rains but also typhoons, said to be caused by sea dragons.

### The dragon and the tiger

In Japan the dragon, Tatsu, embodies the turbulent spirit of nature. Thunderstorms and earthquakes are caused by its constant conflict with the tiger, the symbol of physical nature.

### Python and Apollo

For the ancient Greeks,
Delphi was the centre of the world, its powerful
earth energy manifested in the dragon Python.
The god Apollo slew the beast, fixing its energy
forever at Delphi, where it inspired the oracles
uttered by the Pythia, the priestess of Python.

### Coatlicue

The Aztec earth goddess Coatlicue ("Serpent Skirt") has two
dragon heads, symbolizing both the benign and malevolent
aspects of nature. She wears a dress of rattlesnakes and a
necklace of severed hands and hearts with a skull as centre-
piece – gruesome tokens of nature's supremacy over humanity.

# The Chinese dragon

In China, dragons are said to determine the shape of the landscape, and buildings are positioned in relation to their energy. The Chinese dragon is fierce but rarely malevolent: it represents the East, the sun, and the bounty of the land. The blue Heavenly Dragon guards the celestial mansions of the gods.

### The imperial dragon

Each emperor was seen as the incarnation of the dragon Yu, the mythical founder of the ancient Xia dynasty. Long, the five-clawed dragon, was the emblem of imperial power and its use by commoners was forbidden on pain of death. Members of the imperial family were buried along "dragon lines", powerful paths of dragon energy.

**The pearl of wisdom**
The dragon Long is often
depicted clutching a fiery
pearl in its claws. This may
represent the moon as
a source of fertility,
but for Taoists and
Buddhists it is the
"pearl which grants
all desires", standing
for wisdom and spiritual
enlightenment.

**Mang, the four-clawed dragon**
The dragon Mang represents temporal power. Unlike its imperial
and heavenly relatives, it has four claws: in China, four is the number
of the earth, while five is an auspicious number of great mystical
significance. The earliest Chinese dragons, from which the
Japanese dragon (see page 6) is derived, had three claws.

# The lord of fertility

$A$s controllers of the rains and dwellers in the soil, dragons are closely associated with the fruitfulness of the land. When the Greek fertility goddess Demeter sent the prince Triptolemos to bring corn and agriculture to the world, she lent him a chariot drawn by dragons, emblems of her authority.

**The dragon's roar**

The dragon (above) occurs frequently in Celtic lore. One legend tells how two fighting dragons roared so loudly that women became infertile and the land barren. Fruitfulness returned when King Lud of Britain made the dragons drunk on mead and slew them.

**The rainbow dragon**

Australian Aborigines believe that a great serpent-dragon caused a flood which swept away the primordial world and gave rise to the present people and landscape. The creature is manifested in the rainbow and heralds the onset of the rainy season.

### Jason and the dragon

An oracle declared that the soil of Iolcus in
Greece would never prosper until the golden
fleece of a magic ram, watched over by a
never-sleeping dragon, was brought from
Colchis. Aided by the goddess Athene, who
saved him from the creature's jaws, the hero
Jason slew the dragon and stole the fleece.

### The dragon of Osiris

The imperial dragon of ancient Egypt represents
the god Osiris, lord of the dead and ruler of the
underworld. Every year, it was believed, the
dragon caused the Nile to flood, bringing water
to the dry fields.

# The lord of darkness

Dragons often inhabit underground or submarine regions, and are associated in many cultures with dark, sinister forces. In Christian countries, their reptilian nature links them with the serpent, the form taken by evil in the story of Adam and Eve. Eastern Native American traditions tell of horned underwater dragons that cause drownings.

### The battle of Seth and Apep
After sunset, the Egyptian sun god Ra came under attack from the great serpentine dragon Apep, lord of darkness and chaos. The god Seth fought off the dragon (above).

### Marduk and Tiamat
In Sumerian myth, the dragon Tiamat (left) embodied primeval dark forces. She led a horde of monsters against the deities of order and was slain by the god Marduk.

### St Michael, captain of hosts

According to the Book of Revelation, the Archangel Michael, leader of the heavenly host, fought and killed a dragon that was the incarnation of Satan (left). The dragon is sometimes depicted with seven heads, symbols of the seven deadly sins.

### The power of the cross

St Margaret of Antioch (left), a 3rd-century virgin martyr, was awaiting execution for rejecting the advances of the Roman governor, when she was devoured by the Devil in the form of a dragon. She burst from its body by making the sign of the cross.

### Muhammad and the dragon

In Islam, Iblis (Satan) may take the form of a serpent or dragon. The Prophet Muhammad (right, in white veil), once pacified a giant dragon infesting the site of a new temple.

# The terrible guardian

Since antiquity, dragons have been depicted as monstrous guardians, especially of treasure. In Greek myth the golden apples of the Hesperides were watched over by the dragon Ladon, and the Norse dragon Fafnir guarded a huge horde of gold. The dragon was also the guardian of kings: the Saxon invaders of Britain fought under the banner of the white dragon.

### Perseus and Andromeda
Greek myth relates how Andromeda, daughter of King Cepheus, was chained to a rock in the sea off Joppa (modern Jaffa, Israel) to placate a sea dragon that was ravaging the kingdom. Mounted on the winged horse Pegasus, Perseus killed the monster and rescued Andromeda – then married her.

### The jaws of Hell
Christian artists often depict the giant head of a dragon as the guardian of the way to Hell. The souls of the damned must pass through the dragon's jaws on their way to eternal punishment.

### St George and the dragon

Despite the fame of England's patron saint, there is little evidence for the existence of St George, a 4th-century martyr who is said to have rescued a maiden from a rapacious dragon (above). The legend takes place near Joppa, and may be a christianized version of the myth of Perseus and Andromeda. It also echoes the legend of St Michael.

### Uther's dream

In Welsh legend it is said that after the warrior Uther dreamed of a fiery red dragon, he took the name Pendragon ("Chief Dragon"), and adopted the red dragon as his symbol. It was later borne by his son, King Arthur, and became the badge of Wales.

# The dragon of the mind

Some psychologists view the dragon as a symbol of profound human concerns. As a creature with both benign and sinister attributes, it may stand for the essential duality of the human mind, the interplay of light (the conscious) and dark (the subconscious). In dreams, it may represent the fear of death.

**The dragon in the labyrinth**
The labyrinth symbolizes the complex entirety of the human psyche. The dragon at its centre (above) can be said to represent the psychological archetype called the Shadow: the sinister alter ego which lurks deep in the subconscious.

**Visions of St Anthony**
When St Anthony of Egypt (c. AD 251–356) lived as a hermit, he had alarming visions of dragons, monsters and earthly temptations. He overcame these, seen by his followers as the work of the Devil, through prayer and acts of penitence.

### The dragon in the tower

The myth of the hero who rescues the
maiden from the dragon in the tower
has been interpreted as a metaphor for
a man's achievement of sexual maturity.
The phallic tower stands for the male
sexual persona. In liberating the maiden
(his anima, the female aspect of the male
psyche) from the dragon (the regressive
hold of his mother), he becomes able to form
mature relationships with women.

### Amphisbaena

The amphisbaena is a dragon with
two heads, which are often depicted
fighting one another. The creature
represents inner conflict, either
some current dilemma or, on a more
profound level, the confrontation
between the conscious self, the Ego,
and the destructive power of the Shadow
(see opposite page).

# Creatures of the skies

**M**ythical giant birds appear in many cultures as guardians of the skies, symbols of the awesome power of thunder, lightning, wind and rain. As early as the third millenium BC, the Sumerians believed that Zu, the god of storms, took the form of a bird.

### Thunderbird

In Native American tradition, the spirit of thunder manifests itself in the form of the mighty, eagle-like Thunderbird (above). Lightning flashes from its eyes or beak and the beating of its wings is heard as thunderclaps. Anything struck by the creature's lightning is thought to possess strong spiritual power.

### Hamsa

The mount of the god Brahma, Hamsa is a fabulous wild goose or swan that embodies the divine creator spirit. Its flight symbolizes the soul's quest for release.

### Roc

The roc, a huge fabulous bird of Arabian myth, can carry off a whole elephant to feed its young, and the turbulence caused by its wings is the source of the winds.

### Harpy

The Greeks believed that when a person died suddenly, his or her soul was snatched by a Harpy, a vulture-like monster with the face of a hag. The hero Jason rescued a blind old man, Phineus, from Harpies that constantly snatched his food or defecated on it.

### Garuda

Part eagle and part human, the celestial Garuda hatches fully formed from its egg. It is the mount and emblem of the god Vishnu, the protector of humanity. Garuda's particular enemies are the Nagas, the semi-divine serpent race of the underworld.

# Creatures of the waters

**M**ythical creatures often symbolize the hidden dangers of th
turbulent depths. In Jewish and Christian tradition, the chaotic
forces of the deep are embodied in Leviathan, the largest beast
created by God and so vast that it must eat a fish three miles
long every day. Originally God created two Leviathans,
but destroyed one lest they consume the earth.

### Scylla and Charybdis
These monsters were believed by the ancient
Greeks to live on either side of the
straits between Italy and Sicily.
When the sea god Poseidon fell in love
with the nymph Scylla, his
jealous wife Amphitrite
turned her into a beast
with six heads, each
containing three rows of teeth.
Scylla would snatch sailors from
passing ships. Charybdis,
the offspring of Poseidon's
adultery with the earth
goddess Gaia, resembled
a giant whirlpool. Three
times a day she sucked in water
with enough force to swallow a ship.

### Kraken

The kraken, which lived off Scandinavia and resembled a giant squid or crab, was said to be so great that it was often mistaken for an island. When it rose to the surface it drove shoals of fish before it, which meant rich pickings for fishermen – unless they strayed too close to the monster.

### Makara

The most common aquatic monster of Hindu myth, the makara resembles a fish with the legs and head of a mammal, such as an elephant. As the mount of the water god Varuna, it symbolizes the divine power of the waters.

### Mermaid and merman

The mermaid, a creature said to be part woman and part fish, is reputed to have a beautiful voice but no soul – unless she marries a human that truly loves her. Her male counterpart is the merman.

## Creatures of fire and light

The eagle and the lion have been revered since ancient times as incarnations of fire and solar energy. As the agent of renewed life and transfiguration, the sun is most famously symbolized by the phoenix (right). Every 500 years, by one account, the bird flew to Heliopolis in Egypt to be burnt on the altar of the sun god – only to emerge from the ashes, miraculously revived.

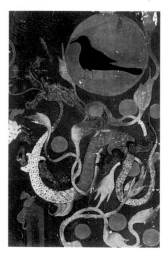

### The crow in the sun

An ancient Chinese belief claims that the spirit of the sun is a large crow, an idea possibly derived from the observation of sunspots. The crow sometimes has three legs, symbolizing sunrise, noon, and sunset.

### Gryphon

Marrying the forms of the eagle and the lion, the majestic gryphon shares their noble qualities of dignity, courage and wisdom. It was said to build its nest of gold, the solar element, and in antiquity it was sacred to Apollo, the god of light.

### Pegasus

The flying horse Pegasus sprang from the blood of the monster Medusa and soared to the bright peak of Olympus, the home of the gods. Pegasus represents the light of heaven and the transcendence of our higher natures over base instincts.

### Salamander

The Romans believed that asbestos was the wool of the salamander, a legendary reptile that was impervious to fire. In medieval bestiaries, it symbolized righteousness unaffected by lust or passion.

# Creatures of darkness

The shadowy spirits of night and darkness appear all the more sinister when manifested in the form of fantastic creatures. Real animals are often credited with supernatural powers because of their nocturnal habits: the Navajo claim that owls are spirits of the dead that travel between this world and the next.

### Celestial demon

The ferocious Tian Gou (Heavenly Dog) of Chinese legend lives in the night sky, occasionally leaping to earth to bring famine and flood and to devour newborn children. Tian Gou causes meteors and comets as well as eclipses, which occur when he devours the sun or moon.

### Lord of night

The largest and fiercest cat of the Americas, the jaguar (left) was an emblem of darkness, death and war. The Maya believed that between sunset and dawn the sun god Ahau Kin travelled through the underworld as the terrifying Jaguar God, lord of the night.

### Werewolf

The werewolf, the man or woman who changes at night into a savage wolf, is a chilling symbol of the bestial instincts lurking beneath the veneer of human civilization. In Slav tradition, those born with a caul (a thin membrane covering the head) were marked as werewolves: the caul was often preserved as a talisman against evil.

### Minotaur

Pasiphaë, the wife of King Minos of Crete, had intercourse with a bull and gave birth to the monstrous Minotaur. The violent creature, part bull and part man, was locked away in the dark Labyrinth — a symbol of our most repressed instincts and desires.

## Creatures of ice and snow

Creatures associated with winter often possess a dual significance, reflecting the season's ambivalence as a time of barrenness that possesses the potential for new growth. For Arctic peoples, reindeer or caribou are powerful spirit beings, emblems of death and of the promise of renewed life – symbolized by the annual loss of their antlers in winter and their subsequent regrowth.

### Mammoth

The Evenk people of Siberia believe that the mammoth, the frozen remains of which are discovered in the ground, is a creator spirit of the lower world. As it walked, rivers sprang up in its tracks, and wherever it lay down, lakes arose. It pulled up mud from the primeval waters to form the land.

### Footprints in the snow

Yetis, the elusive "abominable snowmen" of the Himalayas, are believed to be either guardian spirits associated with the Buddhist god of mercy, or else beings into which peoples' souls transmigrate after death. The creature is said to leave large footprints and has been described by locals as "less than human, more than ape".

**Capricornus**
The fish-tailed goat, symbol
of the winter solstice and
tenth sign of the zodiac, is of
ancient Babylonian origin: it is
associated with Ea, the god of
the deep waters. The goat and
fish symbolize the vital energy
respectively of the earth and
water. Together they represent
the end and beginning of the
annual creative cycle, marked
when the winter sun reaches
its lowest point.

## Keepers of wisdom

**A**nimal beings are frequently respected as the possessors of wisdom or the repositories of special lore. In China, intelligent youngsters were once nicknamed "children of the *ky-lin*", a single-horned beast also known as the Chinese unicorn. Its appearance was said to presage the birth of an eminent philosopher.

**Salmon of Knowledge**
Irish legend tells of a salmon that acquired supernatural wisdom through eating the nuts of nine hazel trees. The hero Finn ate this salmon and received the gift of poetic inspiration and prophecy.

**Sphinx**
The Egyptian sphinx, a hybrid of human, bird and lion, was an emblem of the spiritual power of the Pharaoh. For the Greeks the creature (left) was a keeper of secret knowledge that destroyed those who could not answer her riddles.

**The herald of wisdom**
The Feng Huang, or Chinese phoenix (right), was the gentlest and wisest of all birds, and the personal symbol of the empress. It was believed that, like the *ky-lin*, the bird would appear prior to the birth of a great philosopher.

## Simurgh

The benign Simurgh of Persia (left) was a fabulous bird possessing divine wisdom and powers of prophecy. It suckled its young, like a mammal – demonstrating its link with both the heavens and the earth.

### Chiron the Centaur

The Centaurs, a race with the bodies of horses and the torsos of men, were renowned in ancient Greece for being brutish and licentious. Chiron was an exception: cultured, wise and kindly, he was the friend of the god Apollo and the tutor of several Greek heroes, including Achilles (above).

### The dogs of Fo

Chinese Buddhists revere the little dog of Fo (or lion-dog) as a guardian of the law and a symbol of the Buddha's enlightenment. The animal (right) rests one paw on a ball, possibly the Pearl of Wisdom.

## Enchanters and bewitchers

Legend and folklore abound
with tales of people enchanted
by fabulous beings such as the
Sirens of Greek myth (right),
malign creatures with the bodies
of birds and the heads of women.
They lived on an island and
would lure unsuspecting sailors
onto sharp rocks with their
irresistible, hauntingly
beautiful song.

**Song of the Sirin**

The Sirin of Slav folklore (left) is a
fabulous bird with a woman's head.
It may derive from the Greek Siren,
although it is a benevolent creature: the
good are rewarded for their righteous
lives by hearing the Sirin's entrancing
song, which grants them a blissful death.

### Basilisk

Travellers in the deserts
of the Near East once
went in fear of the
Basilisk or Cockatrice,
a yellow-eyed monster described as part
venomous serpent and part cockerel. It
was so powerfully malevolent that it could
drive people mad or kill with its stare.

### Melusine the fair

According to medieval French legend,
Count Raymond de Lusignan was
spellbound by the beautiful Melusine,
a fairy's daughter. She agreed to marry
him, but made him promise never to
see her on Saturdays. Overcome with
curiosity, Raymond spied on his wife
as she bathed one Saturday and saw
that on this day she became, from the
waist down, a glistening azure serpent.
Knowing her secret was out, Melusine
uttered three shrieks and flew out of
the window, never to be seen again.

## Heroes and tricksters

**M**yth and folklore frequently ascribe fabulous qualities to real animals. They may be heroic characters, such as the praying mantis (which in southwestern Africa is said to have brought fire to humanity), or tricksters, noted for their mischievous or humorous activities. The same animal can be both hero and trickster: the hare, regarded almost universally as a crafty joker, is revered by the Winnebago people of North America as the bringer of their curing rituals.

### Malu

Malu the red kangaroo was one of the many ancestral heroes who, according to Aboriginal myth, journeyed across Australia in the primeval period called Dreamtime. On his journey from the Kimberley mountains in the northwest to the centre of the continent, Malu left caves, rocks and creeks to mark the places where he hunted, camped or fought.

### The hare in the moon

The hare, like the rabbit, is associated with fertility and vitality. The Chinese equivalent of the man in the moon is a hare (left) that continually mixes the elixir of eternal life with its pestle and mortar.

## Coyote

One popular trickster in Native American folklore is Coyote, whose cunning, swiftness and appetite resemble that of the fox in the Old World. Coyote is also revered as a creator. According to the Navajo he was the bringer of seeds to humanity, and the Lakota credit him with the creation of the horse.

## Hanuman

Hindus revere the monkey Hanuman (above) as the paragon of devoted service to the god Rama and his wife Sita. When Sita was abducted by the evil king Ravana and imprisoned on the island of Lanka, Hanuman leapt over the sea to find her and ravage Ravana's kingdom.

## Raven

Until he stole fire from heaven and gave it to humans, the raven was a white bird, say the Tsimshian people of British Columbia. To punish him for his theft, the gods scorched him black.

# A family of monsters

**M**onsters appear often in classical mythology as representatives of the untamable forces that face humanity. Their adversaries are great heroes, such as Perseus and Herakles. Some of the most famous creatures sprang from the incest of two monsters, Echidna (right) and her brother Typhon, a hundred-headed giant. Echidna and Typhon were themselves products of an earlier incestuous coupling, between the earth goddess Gaia and her brother Tartarus, god of darkness.

**The Nemean Lion**

The hide of the monstrous lion of Nemea was impervious to any pointed weapon, so Herakles made a huge club and beat the lion senseless before strangling it. He skinned it with its own claws and wore its pelt to render himself invulnerable.

**The Lernaean Hydra**

A great nine-headed serpent, the Hydra infested a swamp near Lerna in southern Greece. Whenever Herakles cut off one of its heads, two more grew in its place. He overcame the problem by cauterizing each neck as he decapitated it.

### Echidna

Echidna had the upper body of a nymph and the lower body of a repulsive serpent. She coupled with Typhon to produce the Nemean Lion, the Hydra, Cerberus and the Chimera. Echidna was also sometimes said to be the mother of the Sphinx (which plagued the city of Thebes), Orthus (a monstrous two-headed dog) and Ladon (the dragon of the Hesperides).

### Cerberus

Cerberus, the guardian of the entrance to the underworld, was a huge, ferocious dog with three heads. Herakles wrestled with Cerberus and dragged him off to show the King of Tyrins, before sending the dog back to the underworld unharmed.

### Chimera

The fire-breathing Chimera was so outlandish that it came to symbolize anything fantastical or non-existent: it had the body of a lion, a goat's head on its back, and a serpent for a tail. It was slain by the hero Bellerophon mounted on the winged horse Pegasus.

# The elusive unicorn

Usually described as white and resembling a horse, but with cloven hooves and a single twisted horn in its forehead, the unicorn was associated with the moon as an emblem of purity, chastity and femininity. Its horn was said to detect poison and render it harmless. The unicorn shunned all human company except that of a virgin maiden, in whose lap it would gently lay its head.

### The mystic hunt

In medieval Europe the unicorn hunt (above) symbolized the Annunciation, when the Archangel Gabriel told the Virgin Mary that she was destined to bear the Son of God. The hunter (Gabriel) and his hounds (often called Mercy, Truth, Justice and Peace) pursue the unicorn (Christ) into the lap of the Virgin, allowing Him to be claimed for humanity.

### The unicorn and the hart

Like the lion, the hart or stag represents masculine energy, in contrast to the feminine energy of the unicorn. But the hart and the unicorn are not adversaries: they are both symbols of Christ and are said to be the joint guardians of the Tree of Life. In the Middle Ages the hart was believed to rejuvenate itself by sniffing up snakes and swallowing them.

### The lion and the unicorn

Depicted together, the unicorn (symbolizing the lunar and feminine) and the lion (the solar and masculine) represent the union of opposites. They are often portrayed as enemies: in one ancient tale, the lion leaps behind a tree to avoid being speared by the unicorn's horn, which becomes embedded in the tree. The trapped unicorn is then killed by its former prey.

# Beasts of heraldry

O riginally a simple means of identification in combat, heraldry developed into a highly complex symbol system for expressing the character, position and aspirations of the bearer of a coat of arms. Animals feature prominently among heraldic symbols. Most common is the lion, a universal marker of positive qualities such as courage, power and justice, especially when it is depicted *rampant* (rearing up defiantly). As the king of beasts it is often the badge of monarchs.

**Wyvern**
The wyvern, a winged dragon with two legs, symbolizes pestilence and war. The lion rampant stands here for military prowess and fortitude.

## Lion of the spirit
On the arms of Cambridge University (right), the combination of the Christian cross and the lion *regardant* (looking out at the viewer) symbolize intellectual enlightenment and the watchfulness of the spirit.

### Leopard

The heraldic leopard differs little from the heraldic lion. However, it also stands for vigilance, from an old belief that its spots were eyes.

### Elephant

Emblems of strength, wisdom and fidelity, the elephants (above) are also a play on words: the arms are those of a family called Oliphant.

### Stag

The stag draws the chariot of Time and the winged horse (Pegasus) represents a striving for excellence. They are also symbols of swiftness. The lion represents the spirit of enterprise.

### Lyon-poisson

The hybrid lyon-poisson ("lion-fish") on the arms of the old East India Company draws symbolism from each of its components: it stands for the might of the oceans and fortitude at sea.

# Acknowledgments

The publishers are grateful to the following for permission to
reproduce their photographs:

Key: b: bottom c: centre l: left r: right t: top

**Page 5**: The Victoria & Albert Museum, London/E.T. Archive, London;
**6**: The Victoria & Albert Museum/The Bridgeman Art Library, London;
**7**: Charles Walker Collection, London/Images, London; **8**: Bonham's,
London/The Bridgeman Art Library; **9**:(tr) Christie's, London/The
Bridgeman Art Library; **9**:(br) Private Collection/Werner Forman Archive,
London; **10**: (*Tjapaltjarri Ceremony*, 1989, by Clifford Possum) Rebecca
Hossack Gallery, London; **12**: Lambeth Palace Library, London/The
Bridgeman Art Library; **13**:(tl) Upton House, Warwickshire/National Trust
Photographic Library, London; **13**:(br) Museum of Turkish and Islamic Arts,
Istanbul/E.T. Archive; **14**:(cl) (*Perseus and Andromeda*, by F. Leighton) Walker
Art Gallery, Liverpool/The Bridgeman Art Library; **14**:(br) Lambeth Palace
Library/The Bridgeman Art Library; **15**: (*St. George and the Dragon*, by P.
Uccello) The National Gallery, London; **16**: (*The Temptation of St. Anthony*, by
M. Schongauer) Gabinetto Disegni e Stampe, Uffizi, Florence/The
Bridgeman Art Library; **17**:(bl) Glasgow University Library/E.T. Archive;
**17**:(cr) Biblioteca Estense, Modena/E.T. Archive; **18**: The Victoria & Albert
Museum/The Bridgeman Art Library; **21**:(cr) Private Collection,
Khajmaha/Charles Walker Collection/Images; **21**:(br) Palacio de los
Fronteira, Lisbon/E.T. Archive; **22**:(tr) Bodleian Library, Oxford/
E.T.Archive; **22**:(bl) The British Museum, London/The Bridgeman Art
Library; **23**:(cr) Lambeth Palace Library/The Bridgeman Art Library; **25**:(tr)
Charles Walker Collection/Images; **25**:(bl) (*The Minotaur*, by G.F. Watts) The
Tate Gallery, London/The Bridgeman Art Library; **27**: Glasgow University
Library/E.T. Archive; **28**: The British Museum/Charles Walker Collection/
Images; **29**:(tr) (*Achilles and Chiron*, fresco, Herculaneum) Museo Nazionale,
Naples/Scala, Florence; **30**:(tr) (*The Siren*, by A. Point) Barry Friedman,
New York/The Bridgeman Art Library; **31**: Charles Walker Collection/
Images; **32**:(cl) Private Collection, Prague/Werner Forman Archive; **32**:(bl)
Private Collection/Michael Holford, London; **33**:(tl) The Victoria & Albert
Museum/The Bridgeman Art Library; **33**:(br) The National Museum of
Man, Ottawa/Werner Forman Archive; **36**: The Fitzwilliam Museum/The
Bridgeman Art Library; **37**:(tr) Charles Walker Collection/Images; **37**:(bl)
Musée Cluny, Paris/The Bridgeman Art Library; **38**:(t) John Lucas-
Scudamore Collection/The Bridgeman Art Library; **38**:(b) Guildhall Library,
London/The Bridgeman Art Library; **39**:(tl) Guildhall Library/The
Bridgeman Art Library; **39**:(tr) National Library of Scotland, Edinburgh/The
Bridgeman Art Library; **39**:(bl) P.B. Whitehouse Collection/The Bridgeman
Art Library; **39**:(br) Guildhall Library/The Bridgeman Art Library.